SPROUTING RECIPES DIET

Sprouts for weight loss

Gloria Mitchell

By Antonio Tagliafierro

Preface

This book is based on research and all topics covered are for purpose of information and education. This is not a medical or therapy book and all the topics that are related to field of medicine are based on research.

The book is a combination of sprouting basics such as growing sprouts, benefits of sprouts etc. and delicious recipes using the sprouted seeds, beans or grains. Chapter 1 talks a bit about basic details and history of sprouting to make it understandable for beginners. Next chapters include details about choosing seeds for sprouting, different methods for growing sprouts, benefits of growing sprouts at home, benefits of using sprouts in diet, medical and nutritional facts related to sprouting and then the delicious recipes of different sprouted seeds, beans, and grains. This book is a full package for beginners who are health conscious and want to add sprouts in their diet.

Sprouting guide for beginners

The germinating seeds with growing little shoots are called sprouts and the process is called sprouting. Mankind has known sprouting since ancient times and today we have many methods for sprouting different seeds, beans, and grains. The basic technique for sprouting is very simple. The seeds, beans, or grains are soaked in water to start germinating process. The chemical changes start occurring and enzymes are produced. These enzymes allow growing sprouts to avail all nutrients present in the seed for growth. The complex carbs and proteins are broken down into simple amino acids and sugars which are then used in growth. As a result, we have sprouts in a few days.

The germination of seeds transforms the shape of the seed as well as its nutrition. It is studied that during germination, the Vitamin synthesis is 6 to 10 times greater as compared to the levels in non-germinated seeds. Endogenous enzymes help in absorbing more proteins, fats, and starches during germination.

Talking with history

The history of sprouting and its uses by mankind takes us a long time back. History books tell us that ancient Chinese used to eat bean sprouts in their regular diet some 3000 B.C. Not only in diet, but they also used sprouts for therapeutic purposes and the evidence is a book that was written by the Chinese emperor of that time. He had studied and concluded that the sprouted beans could be used in the cure of bloating, nervous system problems, muscular cramps, digestive diseases, and weakened lungs.

History tells us that the use of sprouts is older than Bible. However, it passed through many evolutionary processes and adopted many improvements with time. In the 16th century, work on Chinese herbs discussed the medicinal and therapeutic importance and value of sprouts. The study found that sprouts can be used in reducing inflammation, curing dropsy and rheumatism, getting a laxative effect, and developing the body.

People of Asian mountainous regions used to survive on sprouts during long winter seasons. When they were short of food during winter, they ate sprouts to get vitamins, enzymes, and energy.

However, the history of sprouts in the West is not similar to the East. British sailor Captain James Cook first tested the antiscorbutic properties of sprouts. Scorbutic is also known as scurvy is caused by a lack of Vitamin C and reduces the resistance to infections. It also causes weakness, weight loss, swollen joints, bleeding gums, loosened teeth, and bleeding under the skin in severe cases. These symptoms were normally found in ship's crew during long voyages and it was a type of culture to lose half of the crew during long voyages due to Scurvy. But Captain James never lost any man in his crew, the reason was his study on sprouts and the way he used sprouts for Vitamin C. James and his crew used a specially formulated malt made by cooking sprouted beans at a very low temperature for a longer time. On the other hand, British Navy tried a lot of measures to save the lives of the crew but nothing succeeded. After all, it was found that the only solution and cure to scurvy during voyages is sprouts.

A British doctor John Wiltshire experimented on 60 patients with Scurvy. He wanted to test the scope of sprouts in medicine especially in the cure of scurvy. In this experiment, one group of patients was fed 4 ounces of fresh lemon juice daily and the other group was fed four ounces of sprouted haricot beans. After a month, it was found that patients who were fed sprouts showed a greater rate of improvement. Moreover, the treatment of scurvy using sprouts was found to be less expensive.

During 1938, Scurvy and Famine spread in British India due to crop failures and food shortages. As a result, thousands of people died due to scurvy. To control the situation, a plan was implemented in 1940 to stop the death toll. Each of over 200,000 people was given an ounce of dried sprouted grain or chickpeas twice a week. Within four months, there were no reported cases of scurvy.

Sprouts not only supply Vitamin C to prevent scurvy but they also provide a great number of proteins to maintain health. During world war 2, Researches felt fear of food shortage during the war. So, they came up with an alternative. Researchers suggested sprouted seeds, beans, and grains as an alternative.

The use of sprouts in the diet has been increasing with time. According to a study by O.B. Hesterman and L.R Teuber at the University of California at Davis, people in the USA are eating more sprouts than ever before.

Today you can find different sprout seeds or beans in any supermarket nearby. Sprouting is also getting popular as a new form of farming business. Different types of domestic machines are available to grow sprouts at home. And the list goes on and on.

Benefits of Sprouting

Sprouts increase the levels of minerals and vitamins in the ingredients, including vitamin D. In the book, Diet and Nutrition - A Holistic Approach, author Rudolf Blentin explains that most gas-producing starch can be eliminated by sprouts. Fruits also increase the protein content and shorten the cooking time of beans. During the sprouting process, some of the starch stored in the flowers is used to make small leaf and root links and to make vitamin C. Here are some health benefits that will convince you to sprout more often.

Helps to lose weight

Sprouts are an excellent food to help you lose weight. They have a lot of nutrients but they do not have enough calories which means you can use sprouts without worrying about weight scale. In addition, sprouts contain a lot of fiber which makes you feel full for a long time. It also prevents the release of appetite hormone, ghrelin

Our brain points to overeating

Lists of sprouts for weight loss

There are several types of sprouts that can be enjoyed as part of a weight loss journey. Let's take a look at how you can add sprouts to your diet:

1.Peanut bean sprouts

Peanuts or green sprouts are very popular in Asia. They contain 20 to 24% highly digestible protein and are low in calories. They also contain insoluble fiber and bio-auto compounds that are essential for weight loss.

2. Alfalfa sprouts

There are no sprouts that can beat the nutritional value of alfalfa sprouts in terms of weight loss. Of these, 100 g contains 23 calories, 4 g of protein, and 2 g of fiber. The insane taste of these sprouts makes them great to eat with roasted seeds or to fill in a sandwich.

3. Mung bean sprouts

Mung bean is a powerhouse of macro and micronutrient. They are loaded with high quality protein and digestive fiber that provide warmth and promote weight loss. Cook these sprouts to make curry or a delicious breakfast.

Helps in digestion

Sprouts have an unusually high content of live enzymes. These enzymes further help boost your metabolic process and improve the chemical reactions inside the body, especially when it comes to digestion. Enzymes help break down food efficiently and increase the absorption of nutrients by digestion. Sprouts also contain a lot of dietary fiber which regulates digestion. Fiber increases stool, which makes it easier to pass through the digestive tract.

Studies show that when seeds germinate, the amount of fiber in them increases and becomes more available. For example, in one study, grains were allowed to germinate for five days, which contained 133% more fiber than sprouted grains.

In another, pomegranate-crushed beans increased their fiber content by 226% until their sprouts were 5 mm long. Encryption specifically increases the amount of insoluble fiber, a type of fiber that helps the stool form and pass through the intestines, reducing the chances of constipation. Also, sprouts appear to reduce the amount of gluten found in sprouts, which can make them easier to digest, especially for people who are sensitive to gluten.

Helps reduce acidity

Sprouts are becoming alkalis in the body. They help regulate and maintain your body's pH level by lowering acid levels. It is known that many diseases, including cancer, are associated with excess acid in the body. Add sprouts to your salad to ensure less acidity than citrus fruits.

Delicious ways to use sprouts in the diet

Sprouts are more than just a garnish (although they make great garnishes)! They are very versatile.

Sprouts are great on any kind of salad greens. They also work well with cereal salads! This is a great way to get a taste of spicy radish without having to worry about looking radish.

Great as a topper for sprouted toast! The avocado toast scrambled the balsamic roasted strawberry toast with the egg toast or buckwheat.

The bowls are great food, and they are strewn with piles of different toppings that are much better than that. Sprouts will make a huge addition to these toasted farrowed grain bowls with roasted winter veggies, or a veggie bowl made with lemon-flossed vinegar.
Sprouts can even be made into a salad. They are great with pumpkin seed oil and light vinegar made from fresh citrus juice.

Sprouted beans for topping

You can use mature or less mature bean sprouts for topping your favorite dishes. Pouring a handful of bean sprouts over your favorite salads will give your meal an exceptional taste, nutrition, and look.

Sprouts Salad

Why just topping, you can have a whole nutritionally delicious sprouts salad. Just toss a few chopped vegetables and fruits with sprouted beans and the whole world of taste and health is yours.

Use in soups and stews

Adding sprouts to your soups or stews will add an extra taste and nutrition. Use fresh sprouts or dead ones, taste is going to burst your mind. Don't miss it.

Use as flour

Sprout, then dehydrate beans, then grind into a sprouted bean flour. Then use as a substitute in recipes calling for bean flour.

Best seeds sprout to use for diet

Below is a list of some of the best sprouting seeds and what they taste like so that you can pick the right sprouts for your preferences. You may also want to pick a few and mix them—you can create all sorts of delicious flavor combinations!

Best sprouts for diet

Kidney beans sprouts

Kidney bean is a type of common bean that has a kidney-like shape. Their sprouts are high in protein and low in calories and carbs. One cup (184 grams) of kidney beans bursts.

- Calories: 53
- Carbs: 8 grams
- Protein: 8 grams
- Fat: 1 gram
- Vitamin C: 79% of daily value (DV)
- Folate : 27% of DV
- Iron: 8% DV

These sprouts are also abundant in melanton, a molecule that also prepares your body to regulate the sleep cycle. Melatonin also has antioxidant properties that protect your body from free radicals, which are harmful compounds that can damage cells.

While your body naturally produces melatonin, its production decreases with age. Researchers believe that low levels of age may be linked to health problems as you age.

Numerous studies have linked melatonin intake to a lower risk of chronic diseases, such as type 2 diabetes and heart disease.

A 12-year study of 370 women found that people with low melatonin levels had a significantly higher risk of developing type 2 diabetes. Meanwhile, another study found that rats had a 16% increase in their blood melatonin levels after they were removed from the kidneys.

Kidney beans are best used. You can boil them, sleep them, or stir fry them, then add them to dishes like stews and noodles.

Lentils

Lentils come in a variety of colors, all of which can be easily encrypted to improve their nutritional value.

- One lentil (77 grams) lentil sprouted pack.
- Calories: 82
- Carbs: 17 grams
- Protein: 7 grams
- Fat: 0.5 grams
- Vitamin C: 14% of DV
- Folate: 19% of DV
- Iron: 14% of DV

Sprouting increases the phenolic content of lentils to 122%. Phenolic compounds are a group of antioxidant plant compounds that can provide anti-cancer, anti-inflammatory, and anti-allergenic properties.

Because of their increased antioxidant capacity, lentil sprouts can lower LDL (bad) cholesterol, high levels of which can increase your risk of heart disease, type 2 diabetes and obesity.

An 8-week study of 39 people with type 2 diabetes found that eating 3/4 cup (60 grams) of lentil sprouts daily lowered triglyceride and LDL (bad) cholesterol levels compared to the control group. Increases HDL (good) cholesterol.

Kidney fruit. Unlike sprouts, lentil sprouts can be enjoyed both cooked or raw. Try them on your favorite salad or sandwich, or add them to soups or steamed veggies.

They are rich in thymine, an important B vitamin for neurotransmitter balance. An interesting fact is that dried lentils are deficient in cysteine and methionine, two essential amino acids. Lentil sprouts, on the other hand, have increased levels of all amino acids, including cysteine and methane, making it an important vegetarian source of complete protein.

Pea sprouts

Pea sprouts are notable for their somewhat sweet taste. Both green and yellow peas can be seen.

They are highly nutritious, with one cup (120 grams) packing:

- Calories: 149
- Carbs: 33 grams
- Protein: 11 grams
- Fat: 1 gram
- Vitamin C: 14% of DV
- Folate: 43% of DV
- Iron: 15% of DV

Pea sprouts contain twice the amount of folate (B9) as raw peas. Deficiencies in this vitamin can lead to birth defects such as heart and nerve tube defects. Nerve tube defects are found when your baby's spinal cord or the bones around the skull do not develop properly, which can lead to brain or spinal cord exposure at birth.

Studies show that folic acid supplements reduce the incidence of nerve tube disorders in women of childbearing age. Health professionals also recommend folate-rich foods, such as sprouted peas.

Pea sprouts are more tender than most sprouts. They do well in salads with leafy greens, but can also be stirred. Kidney beans sprouts.

Chickpea sprouts

Sprouts are easy to germinate and take 2 days to germinate which is relatively fast. They pack significantly more protein than other sprouts and are full of nutrients. Offer one cup (140 grams) of gram sprouts:

- Calories: 480
  Carbs: 84 grams
  Protein: 36 grams
  Fat: 8 grams
  Vitamin C: 5% of DV

  iron: 40% of DV

  Interestingly, the total content of isoflavones in gram has increased more than 100 times. Isoflavones are a phytoestrogen. A plant-based compound that mimics the role of the hormone estrogen.

Because estrogen levels begin to drop when women reach menopause, eating foods rich in phytoestrogens can help reduce bone symptoms, including osteoporosis and high blood cholesterol levels.

A 35-day study of rats found that daily intake of gram significantly reduced bone loss. Another rat study concluded that daily intake of fresh gram sprouts decreased total cholesterol and triglyceride levels, while HDL (good) cholesterol levels increased. This suggests that gram sprouts may be helpful in preventing heart disease.

Peeled chickpeas can be eaten raw as a quick and nutritious snack or mixed to make raw hummus. They can also be cooked in soup or veggie burgers.

Mung Bean sprouts

Mung Bean sprouts are among the most common bean sprouts. They are derived from peanuts, which are grown in East Asia but are also popular in many Western restaurants and stores.

They have a very low-calorie count, with 1 cup (104 grams) offered:

Calories: 31

Carbs: 6 grams

Protein: 3 grams

Vitamin C: 15% of DV

Folate default: 16% of DV

iron: 5% of DV

Peanuts increase the flavonoid and vitamin C content of peanuts 7 and 24 times, respectively. As a result, their antioxidant properties are enhanced. What's more, some research links these sprouts to the potential counter-benefits of fighting free radical damage.

Similarly, a test tube study treated with this extract in human cells discovered a toxic effect on cancer cells - no harm to healthy cells. Peanuts are a staple of Asian cuisine and are perfect for dishes such as fried rice and spring rolls.

Soybean sprouts

Soybean sprouts are a popular ingredient in many Korean dishes. They have grown up drinking soybeans. One cup (70 grams) soybean sprout pack:

Calories: 85

Carbs: 7 grams

Protein: 9 grams

Fat: 5 grams

Vitamin C: 12% of DV

Folate default: 30% of DV

Iron: 8% DV

Fruits reduce the levels of soybean phytic acid, a nutrient that binds to minerals such as iron, and affects their absorption. For example, sprouted soy milk and tofu contain 59% and 56% less phytic acid, respectively, than non-condensed products.

Therefore, soybean sprouts can make non-ham iron - a type of iron found in plants - that is more available to your body. When your iron levels drop, you can't make enough hemoglobin - the protein in the red blood cells that carries oxygen throughout your body. Iron deficiency can lead to anemia.

A 6-month study of 288 girls with iron deficiency anemia found that people who drank 3 ounces (100 ml) of sprouted soy milk daily had significantly improved ferritin levels, the protein you need. Protects iron in the body. Similarly, a 2-week study of mice found that a soybean sprout supplement increased their hemoglobin levels like that of healthy mice.

Thus, sprouted soybeans can help prevent and treat such anemia. Similarly, further research is guaranteed. Soybean sprouts have a crunchy texture and a nutty flavor. They are usually eaten cooked and are added to casseroles and stews.

Adzuki bean sprouts

Adzuki beans are a small red bean grown in East Asia and are similar to peanuts. One cup (133 grams) serving of Adzuki bean sprouts pack:

Calories: 466

Carbs: 84 grams

Protein: 31 grams

Fat: 1 gram

Vitamin C: 17% of DV

iron: 40% of DV

As with most sprouted beans, Adzuki beans increase their phenolic antioxidant content by 25%. The most prominent phenolic compound in these sprouts is synopic acid. Synopeic acid has a number of health-promoting properties, including blood sugar control and anti-inflammatory, antibacterial, and antacid effects.

Animal studies show that cyano acid lowers high blood sugar levels and makes it more resistant to insulin in mice with diabetes. Nevertheless, it is not clear whether Adzuki bean sprouts have the same effect on humans. Adzuki bean sprouts have a nutty flavor and can be added raw to salads, wraps and smoothies. You can also make them in soup.

Some other tasty sprouts

Sprouted Navy Beans
Sprouted navy beans

Large beans can be hard to grow and have a long germination time, but that doesn't make them any more delicious! Seasoned navy beans (a.k.a. haricot, boston or white pea beans) have a strong texture and are delicious to sprinkle on salads.

Sprouted black beans

When it comes to punching, black beans can work well! Use encoded black beans almost anywhere you use regular black beans, such as tacos, britos or southwestern salads.

Alfalfa

Alfalfa Sprouts are one of the most common types of spice, probably because the taste goes with everything! They are small, crunchy sprouts with a mild flavor. Add these anchovies to a dish to add a little reduction and lots of nutrients.

Beet

Beet sprouts have colorful stems in deep red or mangosteen and bright green leaves, so if you want to add beautiful colored pop to a pot, these are the sprouts for you. Their taste is slightly earthy and very sweet.

Broccoli

Broccoli produces dense, heavy sprouts that have a sweet, spicy taste (slightly like radishes). They don't taste as good as broccoli, but they're a delicious addition to anything that can add a little spice. They are also high in antioxidants in particular, so if you are adding more sprouts to your diet to improve your health, this is a good choice.

Fenugreek

Fenugreek has a bitter taste that, when mixed with other flavors, adds complexity to dishes (consider using it in a spout mix) but is not usually eaten on its own. Fenugreek can help relieve upset stomach, so it is a good choice for people with sensitive tumors.

Green peas

Green pea sprouts are fragrant with a fresh, sweet taste reminiscent of ice peas. They are light and go well with other flavors. These are just some of the goal setting sharewares that you can use. I like to grow them together with peanut sprouts because they have growing time and complementary flavors.

Mustard

Mustard sprouts have a heavy flavor and a spicy cook, like horseradish. A perfect sprout for the spice lover!

Radish

Radish sprouts are very thin, with red dotted leaves. They look as beautiful as garnish. They taste like adult radish, but with less spice.

Full of chlorophyll-supporting cellular function, these sprouts are great for weight loss as they provide a sense of fullness with their spicy flavor and also contain important vitamins for metabolism. They also contain important antioxidant compounds, which increase immunity and reduce inflammation.

Sprouts are an important part of a healthy diet and are often overlooked. The benefits of oxidative stress, reduced inflammation, improved cellular respiration, and detoxification far outweigh the costs involved. Regular consumption of sprouts will not benefit you.

Red clover

The dark green piles of red clover sprouts have a light, earthy taste and a very bad temper. They go well with most flavors, so pile them on all your favorite sandwiches, salads, wraps and bowls.

Red clover sprout is a great source of phytoestrogens and can therefore treat many common symptoms such as temperature instability and bloating, but phytoestrogens are also helpful in treating insomnia and anxiety, Assists in detention difficulties.

Spelt

A nutritious, chewy grain with a flavor is a spelt sprout in the grain. If you want to use sprouts in a wonderful way, you can add sprouts in your morning granola, raw bread recipes, and even cooked cookies.

Sunflower

Sunflower sprouts have dense, succulent leaves with succulent leaves that are very grounded. Sunflower sprouts are usually delicious in dishes - salads, sandwiches, bowls, etc. But their sweet taste also makes them a welcome way to pack some more nutrients into fruit smoothies.

Recipes with sprouting seeds, beans and grains

Delicious Sprout Salad

Time required:

40 minutes, ready to serve in 44 minutes

Ingredients:

- ✓ Chopped onions – 1 cup
- ✓ Peeled and cubed cucumber – 1 cup
- ✓ Potatoes – 1 cup

- ✓ Tomatoes – 1 cup
- ✓ Moong dal sprouts – 2 cups
- ✓ Chopped cilantro – 3 tsp
- ✓ Lemon juice – 1 tsp
- ✓ Chopped green chilies – 2 tsp
- ✓ Cumin powder – 2 tsp
- ✓ Salt and pepper to taste

Instructions:

i. Take a large mixing bowl and transfer sprouts to it. Then add all the chopped ingredients into it and give it a toss to mix. Mix gently by using a fork.

ii. Once mixed, add your favorite seasonings if you like and enjoy the healthy sprout salad.

Green gram sprout salad

Time required:

5 minutes, ready to serve in 10 minutes

Ingredients:

- ✓ Sprouted green gram – ¾ cup
- ✓ Chopped onions – 1 tsp
- ✓ Chopped tomato – 1 small
- ✓ Finely chopped cucumber – ¼ cup
- ✓ Crushed small green chili – 1
- ✓ Coriander leaves – 2 tsp
- ✓ Lemon juice – 1 tsp
- ✓ Chopped coconut - 1tsp
- ✓ Cornflakes – ½ cup
- ✓ Ginger – ¼ inch
- ✓ Fresh mint leaves – 1 sprig

Instructions (For preparing sprouts):

i. Take boiled water in a bowl and let it cool. Then soak green gram or mung beans in the water for about 8 hours.
ii. Drain off the water from sprouts using a paper towel.
iii. Add the prepared sprouts in a container or a jar.
iv. Or place it in a bowl and partially cover it. Then set it in a warm and dark place. Depending on the weather conditions, they sprout.
v. If the cloth dries up, sprinkle some water on the cloth to make the beans moist. Do not pour a lot of water otherwise they begin to rot.
vi. Sprouts will be ready within 6 hours to 2 days.
vii. Instructions (For salad):
viii. Peel and chop the ingredients along with tomatoes and chilies. Rinse the coriander leaves and mint. Chop finely.
ix. Take a bowl and add sprouts to it. Add all the chopped veggies and then sprinkle some salt.
x. Squeeze the lemon juice over the ingredients in the bowl and toss them all.
xi. What now? Your deliciously healthy sprouts salad is ready. Enjoy your meal.

Apple sprouted buckwheat cereal

Time required:

5 minutes for the recipe, 3 days required to prepare sprouts

Ingredients:

- ✓ Sprouted buckwheat – 2 cups
- ✓ Cinnamon powder – 1 tsp
- ✓ Diced apple – 1

✓ Unsweetened dried cranberries – ½ cup

Instructions:

i. Measure 3/4 cup of buckwheat groats into a jar and add just enough water to cover the buckwheat. Allow the jar to sit in a safe place for 2-3 hours.

ii. Strain the water from the jar. Rinse the buckwheat by filling with a cool water jar and straining again.

iii. Allow the jar to sit for 3 days at room temperature, rinsing 3 times per day Before you use it, rinse the buckwheat one final time.

iv. Cereal

v. Core and dice 1 apple and set aside.

vi. Measure 2 cups of sprouted buckwheat into a bowl then add raw honey, cinnamon, apple, and cranberries. Mix it all and enjoy!

Chocolate Buckwheat Pancakes

Time required:

10 minutes, ready to serve in 25 minutes

Ingredients:

✓ Buckwheat flour – 1 cup
✓ Unsweetened cocoa powder – ½ cup
✓ Baking powder – 1 ½ tsp
✓ Baking soda – ¼ tsp
✓ Sea salt – ¼ tsp
✓ Egg – 1 large
✓ Unsweetened vanilla – 1 ½ cups
✓ Melted coconut oil – ¼ cup
✓ Vanilla extract – ½ tsp
✓ Almond extract – ¼ tsp

- ✓ Honey – 2 tsp
- ✓ Chopped fresh strawberries – for topping

Instructions:

i. Take a bowl and whisk together the bucket wheat flour, cocoa powder, baking powder, baking soda, and salt until well combined.

ii. Take another medium and whisk together the egg, almond milk, coconut oil, vanilla extract, almond extract, and honey until well combined.

iii. Mix the ingredients until combined.

iv. Take a skillet or a pan and put over medium flame. Once heated, pour olive oil in it.

v. Give the batter a quick stir, then scoop / pour about ¼ cup for each pancake into the skillet (as many as you can comfortably fit).

vi. Cook for about 2 to 3 minutes, until small bubbles start to form on the surface (and the edges are starting to look set). Flip the pancakes and continue to cook for another about 1 minute, until golden brown and set.

vii. Serve the pancakes topped with a drizzle of maple syrup (or honey!) and plenty of fresh strawberries!

Kale & caramel with Feta & Mint

Time required:

15 minutes, ready to serve in 30 minutes

Ingredients:

- ✓ Brussels Sprouts
- ✓ Brussels sprouts – 4 cups
- ✓ olive oil – 5 tsp

- ✓ sea salt – ½ tsp
- ✓ fresh thyme leaves removed – 2 sprigs
- ✓ balsamic vinegar – 1 ½ tsp
- ✓ chopped fresh mint leaves – 3 tsp
- ✓ crumbled feta – ¼ cup
- ✓ pomegranate seeds – ¼ cup
- ✓ Pomegranate Roasted Pecans
- ✓ pecan halves – ½ cup
- ✓ olive oil – ½ tsp
- ✓ maple syrup – 1 tsp
- ✓ pomegranate molasses or balsamic vinegar – 1 tsp
- ✓ salt and fresh cracked pepper to taste

Instructions:

i. Preheat oven to 450°F.

ii. Wash and trim bottoms off Brussels sprouts, then slice in half from top to bottom.

iii. Prepare two 12″ cast iron pans, dividing the oil evenly between each. Heat over medium-high flame for about a minute, then divide Brussels sprouts between the two pans, placing cut side down. Keep any stray leaves out of the pans for now—you'll add them in to roast later. Sprinkle with sea salt and fresh thyme leaves.

iv. Cook until the bottoms begin to brown, then add stray Brussels leaves and shake pans gently. Add balsamic vinegar (divided between pans), stir to coat, and place in oven.

v. Let roast for 10 minutes, then check and give another shake. Another 10 minutes, and another check and shake. Remove from oven when outer Brussels sprout leaves are crispy golden brown and sprouts are soft (20-25 minutes total).

vi.   While they roast, mix olive oil, maple syrup, pomegranate molasses or balsamic, and salt and pepper in a bowl. Add pecans, and toss to coat. Place on a baking sheet and add to rack below sprouts for 3-5 minutes. Remove when fragrant. Set aside.

vii.   Serve Brussels sprouts while hot or warm, topped with pomegranate, feta, pecans, and fresh mint.

Sprouted Almond Milk

Time required:

20 minutes, ready to serve in35 minutes

Ingredients:

- ✓ Unsweetened almond milk – ½ cup
- ✓ Fresh lemon juice – 3 tsp
- ✓ Mung bean sprouts – 2 cups
- ✓ Romaine lettuce leaves – 4 ounces
- ✓ Green pea sprouts – ½ cup
- ✓ Tahini – 2 tsp
- ✓ Sea salt – ¼ tsp
- ✓ Frozen pineapple chunks – 5 ounces
- ✓ Ice cubes – a handful

Instructions:

i.   Take a blender and blend all the ingredients in it for about 2 to 3 minutes.

ii.   If a smoothie is too thick, add water to it.

iii.   You can top your smoothie with any toppings you wish.

Stir-Fried Pea Sprouts

Time required:

10 minutes, ready to serve in 15 minutes.

Ingredients:

- ✓ Pea shoots – 500 g
- ✓ Thinly sliced garlic – 2 cloves
- ✓ Cooking oil – 2 tsp
- ✓ Chicken bouillon powder – 1 tsp
- ✓ Salt to taste – ½ tsp

Instructions:

i. Add the oil into the wok using high heat.
ii. Turn the heat down to a medium and throw in the garlic to avoid burning.
iii. Bring the heat up to high and throw in the pea shoots, chicken bouillon powder, and salt.
iv. Stir for 1-2 minutes (or until slightly wilted) then plate immediately.
v. Serve with a bowl of rice and enjoy!

Notes

i. As with every stir fry, make sure the wok is HOT. You don't want to boil the pea shoots and end up with a soggy plate of vegetables.
ii. Dry the pea shoots as best you can before stir-frying. A little moisture is fine, but you need it as dry as possible to avoid steaming it.
iii. Be quick with your hands. Stir vigorously to evenly cook all the pea shoots.
iv. Turn the heat down to low before adding in the garlic to stop any burning. Burnt garlic will add

unnecessary bitterness to this dish. Increase the heat back up to high before adding in the pea shoots.

Healthy Fenugreek sprouts diabetic snack

Time required:

10 minutes, ready to serve in 15 minutes

Ingredients:

- ✓ Fenugreek Seeds, sprouts – 1 cup
- ✓ Peanuts – 1/3 cup
- ✓ Onion finely chopped – 1
- ✓ Tomato, finely chopped – 1
- ✓ Sprig Coriander Leaves – 2 leaves
- ✓ Salt, to taste
- ✓ Black pepper powder – ½ tsp
- ✓ Lemon juice – 1 tsp
- ✓ Chat Masala Powder – ½ tsp

Instructions:

i. To begin making the Fenugreek Sprouts Salad Recipe, we need to have the methi sprouts ready.

ii. You can either use store-bought Fenugreek sprouts or make Sprouts at Home.

iii. You could also soak Fenugreek seeds in water overnight. The next day, drain off the water and tie them in a muslin cloth and keep them in a warm place for 1 day.

iv. After 24 hours, open the cloth and you will see the sprouts.

v. In a mixing bowl, combine the Fenugreek sprouts along with the peanuts, chopped onions and tomatoes, coriander leaves and mix well.

vi. Then Sprinkle some salt, pepper, and chaat masala and a generous squeeze of lemon and stir to combine to make the Fenugreek Sprouts Salad.

vii. Transfer the Fenugreek Sprouts Salad to a platter and serve as a diabetic snack or even as a side dish for lunch.

viii. Serve Fenugreek Sprouts Salad along with Ragi Tawa Paratha, Fenugreek Moong Dal Recipe for a complete Diabetic Snack, lunch, or dinner.

Arugula and Radish sprouts

Time required:

10 minutes, ready to serve in 20 minutes

Ingredients:

- ✓ Organic Arugula – 2 cups
- ✓ Daikon radish sprouts –1 ½ oz.
- ✓ Dried shaved bonito flakes – ¼ cup
- ✓ Extra virgin olive oil – ½ tsp
- ✓ Lemon juice – ½ tsp
- ✓ Coarse sea salt – 1 pinch

Instructions:

i. Gather the ingredients.

ii. If you're using pre-washed, packaged arugula leaves, refresh them by rinsing them with cold water. Drain well to remove excess water, or use a salad spinner to dry the leaves.

iii. Remove kaiware (daikon radish sprouts) from the package and rinse well to remove any loose brown seed shells. Cut off about one inch of the bottom where the sprouts are attached to a piece of cotton. Discard roots.
iv. Prepare the lemon dressing: In a bowl, combine olive oil, lemon juice, and salt. Mix well.
v. In a small bowl, toss together arugula and kaiware. Just before serving, add dried bonito flakes (katsuobushi) and gently toss them together.
vi. Plate the salad mixture into small individual serving plates and drizzle the lemon dressing over the greens. Alternatively, the dressing may be tossed together with the salad ingredients in advance, but a caveat is that the dried bonito flakes will quickly absorb the dressing and wilt.
vii. Serve and enjoy!

Red clover sprouts with mixed beans

Time required:

5 minutes, ready to serve in 10 minutes

Ingredients:

Drizzle

- ✓ Lime juice – 1 lime
- ✓ avocado – 1
- ✓ garlic clove (crushed) – 1 clove
- ✓ water – 25 ml
- ✓ Pinch of salt + pepper

Salad

- ✓ Large handful of little radish & red clover sprouts

- ✓ can of cannellini beans (washed & drained) – 1 can
- ✓ can of kidney beans (washed & drained) – 1 can
- ✓ red pepper (sliced) – 1
- ✓ yellow pepper (sliced) – 1
- ✓ cherry tomatoes (halved) – 6
- ✓ red onion (finely sliced) – 1
- ✓ Handful of coriander
- ✓ Romaine lettuce leaves

Instructions:

i. Place all of the ingredients into the blender and whizz up until smooth.
ii. Combine all of the ingredients (apart from the lettuce leaves) into a mixing bowl and mix until fully combined.
iii. Fill the lettuce leaves with the salad and top off with the avocado drizzle and more sprouts
iv. Serve and enjoy!

Sprouted spelt biscuits

Time required:

10 minutes, ready to serve in 18 minutes

Ingredients:

- ✓ sprouted spelt flour cannot be warm from grinding or will melt the coconut oil – 2 ¼ cups
- ✓ baking soda – ½ tsp
- ✓ baking powder – 1 ½ tsp
- ✓ sea salt – ¾ tsp
- ✓ coconut oil chilled if liquefied at room temp (like during the summer) – 6 tsp

- ✓ raw whole milk OR coconut milk, or nut milk – ¾ cup
- ✓ raw apple cider vinegar or lemon juice – 1 tsp

Instructions:

i. Preheat the oven to 450 degrees Fahrenheit.
ii. In a mixing bowl, combine the flour, baking soda, baking powder, and sea salt.
iii. Add the coconut oil, then cut it into the flour using a pastry cutter or a fork, until the pieces of oil are the size of peas or smaller.
iv. Add the milk (or water) and vinegar mixture.
v. Mix lightly with a wooden spoon to barely combine the ingredients. Don't overmix!
vi. Transfer the dough to a clean, floured surface and roll into a rectangle about 1/2-inch thick.
vii. Using a knife or pizza cutter, cut into 2-inch squares.
viii. Transfer squares to an oiled cookie sheet, leaving space between.
ix. Put the sheet in the oven.
x. Bake for 8 to 10 minutes, until golden brown.
xi. Transfer to a cooling rack.

Recipe notes:

i. Mix the vinegar and milk about 5 to 10 minutes beforehand to create "buttermilk".
ii. Make sure your spelt flour is not warm from grinding or it will melt the coconut oil.
iii. If you don't have sprouted spelt flour, use whole wheat pastry flour (but use 2-1/2 cups) or unsprouted spelt flour.

iv. For soaking instructions, visit the original recipe at The Nourishing Gourmet.

v. These divine biscuits were inspired by Kimi at The Nourishing Gourmet. She starts with whole wheat pastry flour and soaks the dough (sans baking soda, baking powder, and salt) overnight. We converted them to a sprouted dough for a quicker start to finish time.

Sunflower Sprouts Pate

Time required:

20 minutes, ready to serve in 30 minutes

Ingredients:

- ✓ sprouted sunflower seeds – 4 cups
- ✓ lemons, juiced and zested – 2 lemons
- ✓ garlic, roughly chopped – 3 cloves
- ✓ shallot, roughly chopped – 1
- ✓ extra virgin olive oil – ¼ cup
- ✓ fresh parsley leaves – ¼ cup
- ✓ ground pepper – ½ tsp
- ✓ sea salt, or to taste – 1 tsp

Instructions:

i. Place all ingredients in a food processor or high-powered blender. Pulse until all ingredients are roughly chopped. Scrape down the sides and continue to blend until smooth, scraping down the sides of the machine as needed.

ii. Scrape the pâté from the food processor and taste. Add additional salt as needed.

iii.　Serve as a dip or a spread for raw lettuce, nori, or collard wraps.

Black beans sprout soup

Time required:

20 minutes, ready to serve in 30 minutes

Ingredients:

- ✓ coconut oil or lard – 3 tsp
- ✓ onion, diced – 1 medium
- ✓ green pepper, diced – 1
- ✓ garlic, minced – 4 cloves
- ✓ sprouted black beans – 2 cups
- ✓ chicken broth – 5 cups
- ✓ ground cumin – 2 tsp
- ✓ fresh jalapeño, minced – ½
- ✓ Juice of lime – ½ lime
- ✓ Sea salt to taste
- ✓ Sour cream and cilantro for serving

Instructions:

i.　In a Dutch oven over medium heat, melt coconut oil. Sauté the onion and pepper for 5-8 minutes or until softened. Add garlic and cook an additional 2 minutes.

ii.　Mix in sprouted beans, chicken broth, cumin, and jalapeno. Bring to a boil, cover, and turn heat to low. Simmer at least 45 minutes and up to 2 hours, stirring occasionally. Once beans are very tender, remove them from the heat.

iii.　Stir in the lime juice and season to taste with salt. Serve as is or blend using an immersion blender. If a thicker soup is desired, simmer a bit longer, uncovered, until a portion of the liquid cooks off. Stir frequently as beans tend to scorch easily.

iv. Serve hot with sour cream and cilantro as garnish.

Delicious Beet greens

Time required:

10 minutes, ready to serve in 20 minutes

Ingredients:

- ✓ beet greens stem removed – 2 bunches
- ✓ extra-virgin olive oil, or to taste – 1 tsp
- ✓ garlic, minced – 2 cloves
- ✓ crushed red pepper flakes (Optional) – ¼ tsp
- ✓ salt to taste
- ✓ freshly ground black pepper to taste
- ✓ lemons quartered – 2

Instructions:

i. Bring a large pot of lightly salted water to a boil. Add the beet greens, and cook uncovered until tender, about 2 minutes. Drain in a colander, then immediately immerse in ice water for several minutes until cold to stop the cooking process. Once the greens are cold, drain well, and coarsely chop.

ii. Heat the olive oil in a large skillet over medium heat. Stir in the garlic and red pepper flakes; cook and stir until fragrant, about 1 minute. Stir in the greens until oil and garlic are evenly distributed. Season with salt and pepper. Cook just until greens are hot; serve with lemon wedges.

Korean Soybean (Kongnamool)

Time required:

10 minutes, ready to serve in 15 minutes

Ingredients:

- ✓ soybean sprouts – 1 pound
- ✓ soy sauce – 2 tsp
- ✓ sesame oil – ¼ cup
- ✓ Korean chile powder – 2 tsp
- ✓ garlic, minced – 1 ½ tsp
- ✓ sesame seeds – 2 tsp
- ✓ chopped green onion – ¼ cup
- ✓ rice wine vinegar, or to taste – 2 tsp

Instructions:

i. Bring a large pot of lightly salted water to a boil. Add the bean sprouts, and cook uncovered until tender yet still crisp, about 15 seconds. Drain in a colander, then immediately immerse in ice water for several minutes until cold to stop the cooking process. Once the bean sprouts are cold, drain well, and set aside.

ii. Whisk soy sauce, sesame oil, chile powder, garlic, and sesame seeds together in a large bowl. Stir in bean sprouts and toss until well coated with the sauce. Sprinkle with green onions and season with rice wine vinegar. Refrigerate before serving.

Stir-fried Soybean sprouts

Time required:

15 minutes, ready to serve in 25 minutes

Ingredients:

- ✓ Soy Bean Sprouts – 1 lb.
- ✓ Garlic – 2 cloves
- ✓ Sichuan Peppercorn – 1 tsp
- ✓ Dried chilies - 3
- ✓ Sesame oil – 1 tsp
- ✓ Salt

Instructions:

i. Sliced the garlic and cut the dried chili. Rinse the bean sprouts.

ii. In boiling water, briefly blanched the bean sprouts. About 1 minute. Drain the water in a mesh drainer.

iii. Over high heat, fry the garlic, chili, and Sichuan peppercorn until the chili starts to turn dark. About 30 seconds.

iv. Add the blanched bean sprouts and stir fry in high heat for about 1 minute. Do not wait until the sprouts are dark and soggy. Add the sesame oil and salt to taste.

Spicy sprouted Lentils

Time required:

10 minutes for meal, 3 days for sprouts

Ingredients:

- ✓ green lentils – 1 cup
- ✓ water – 3 cups
- ✓ cooked corn – ¼ cup
- ✓ lemon juice – 3 tsp
- ✓ olive oil – 2 tsp
- ✓ salt – 1 tsp

- ✓ cumin – ½ tsp
- ✓ chili powder – ½ tsp
- ✓ curry powder – ½ tsp
- ✓ finely chopped thyme or another herb you like – ¼ cup

Instructions:

i. Soak lentils in a large bowl overnight or for 8-10 hours.

ii. Drain and rinse the lentils. Put them back in the bowl and cover with a kitchen towel. Let it sit for 8 hours.

iii. Shake the bowl or give a gentle stir so that each of the lentils get enough air circulation. Let it sit for another 8 hours.

iv. Repeat this for 2-3 days. You will see sprouts growing on the second day and they get longer on the third day.

v. Keep them refrigerated and use as you need.

To Assemble Everything:

i. Combine sprouted lentils and corn in a bowl.

ii. In a small bowl, whisk together the lemon juice, olive oil, salt, cumin, chili, curry powder and thyme.

iii. Pour it over the sprouted lentils and corn and toss.

iv. Serve it as a salad or use it in sandwiches or soups

Lentils sprout burger

Time required:

20 minutes, ready to serve in 30 minutes

Ingredients:

- ✓ sprouted black, green or brown lentils – 1 ½ cups
- ✓ cooked brown rice – 1 cup
- ✓ walnuts- lightly toasted (or pecans or sunflower seeds) – 1 cup
- ✓ miso paste (or use chickpea miso if GF) – 1 tsp
- ✓ olive oil – 1 tsp
- ✓ whole grain mustard – 2 tsp
- ✓ granulated garlic (or onion) – 2 tsp
- ✓ cumin – 1 tsp
- ✓ coriander – ½ tsp
- ✓ salt – ½ tsp
- ✓ pepper – ½ tsp
- ✓ fresh herbs- scallions, cilantro parsley, basil, etc. – 4 tsp
- ✓ toasted sesame seeds – 3 tsp

Instructions:

i. In the morning, place 1 cup dry whole lentils and 3-4 cups water in a large mason jar and soak all day (8 hours) on the counter.

ii. In the evening, drain well. Turn jar on its side letting lentils spread out a bit and let the lentils continue to sit on the counter overnight. Once you see the tiny tip of the white sprout begin to emerge, they are ready. Generally, takes 24-30 hours.

iii. Place 1 ½ cups of the raw sprouted lentils (drained well) cooked rice, toasted walnuts, miso, oil, mustard, garlic, salt, spices and pepper in the food processor and pulse repeatedly until combined well and becomes a course, sturdy dough. DO NOT OVER PROCESS! You want it course, not smooth, otherwise, it may get pasty!

iv. Taste for salt. If it tastes bland, check that the miso was properly mixed in (give a few stirs with a spoon, look for miso clump and pulse again).

v. Place a piece of parchment on a small sheet pan or large plate. Sprinkle the parchment with sesame seeds.

vi. With wet hands divide dough into four balls and form 4 burgers, about 1 inch thick. Place on the parchment and coating both sides with sesame seeds.

vii. Place in the fridge uncovered while you heat the grill (15 minutes- to firm up)

viii. You can also pan-sear these and finish in a hot oven.

ix. Preheat grill to medium high heat and oven to 400. F Grease the grill. When hot, sear the lentil burgers until generous grill marks appear, about 4-5 minutes on each side, then place in oven to continue warming all the way through, 10 more minutes (or move to cooler part of the grill).

x. At this point, build your burgers, or wrap and freeze for later.

xi. To make quick pickled beets. Bring liquids, sugar, salt and any spices to a simmer in a small pot on the stove. add grated beets and onion. Stir, simmer for a couple minutes before chilling in the fridge.

Sprouted Lentil Salad

Time required:

20 minutes, ready to serve in 30 minutes.

Ingredients:

- ✓ sprouted lentils – 4 cups
- ✓ red onion, minced – ½
- ✓ minced parsley – ¼ cup
- ✓ spinach, chopped into bite-sized pieces – 4 handfuls
- ✓ Roma tomatoes, diced - 2
- ✓ red wine vinegar, to taste – 3 tsp
- ✓ olive oil, to taste – 4 tsp
- ✓ Sea salt to taste
- ✓ cubed or crumbled cheese - 1/2 cup

Instructions:

i. Combine all ingredients except cheese in a large bowl.
ii. Let sit for at least 30 minutes before serving to allow flavors to meld.
iii. Add cheese and serve.

Broccoli sprouts Salsa

Time required:

10 minutes, ready to serve in 15 minutes

Ingredients:

- ✓ broccoli sprouts – 2 cups
- ✓ chopped tomato – 2 cups
- ✓ Juice of lime – 1
- ✓ minced fresh cilantro leaves – ¼ cup
- ✓ finely minced red onion – ¼ cup
- ✓ seeded, chopped jalapeño – ½
- ✓ Sea salt to taste

Instructions:

i. Roughly chop the broccoli sprouts and combine them with all other ingredients in a medium bowl. Mix well and season with sea salt to taste.

ii. Serve atop grilled fish or chicken, as a dip for chips, or with beans and rice for a vegan meal.

Sprouted lentil Tacos

Time required:

10 minutes, ready to serve in 15 minutes

Ingredients:

- ✓ sprouted lentils – 3 cups
- ✓ onion diced – 1
- ✓ extra virgin olive oil – 2 tsp
- ✓ pure water – 2 tsp
- ✓ homemade taco seasoning blend adjust to taste – 2 tsp
- ✓ homemade tortillas
- ✓ toppings of choice

Instructions:

i. In a skillet, sauté an onion, if desired, in olive oil.

ii. When soft, add lentils and a bit of water.

iii. Sprinkle in taco seasoning.

iv. Stir frequently, letting the lentils steam gently until cooked as soft as you prefer.

v. Taste every now and then to adjust seasoning if necessary. Feel free to add more water to help lentils and spices combine.

vi.   Once cooked, add to homemade tortillas with taco toppings of choice, and enjoy!

How to grow sprouts at home?

Jar method

I. Clean your jars and prepare the seeds in a clean area.

ii. Add 1-2 tablespoons of spirited seeds to a wide mason jar. Dip one foot into warm running water, pausing between layers to allow them to dry. Cover the top with a cheesecloth, or some kind of peg mesh: a part of the screen, whatever you can pull on and off the top will be perfect. But sprouts can stick to cheese cloth so it is recommended that they use a special jar with a stainless-steel lid. It also protects the sprouts from rusting (the iron caps become rusty due to moisture) and promotes healthy growth of the sprouts.

iii. Any kind of clear glass jar is perfect for making anchor rout. Old pickle jars, mason pots or other glass containers can reproduce the sprouts. If you still find a metal ring around the mouth of a mason jar, you can use it to hold the mesh sheet in place, or you can use a hair tie, rubber band, or something else to do so. Can use elastic bands. Buying a jar with a stainless-steel lid is the best choice.

iv. If you want to grow microgreens such as arugula, wheat grass, or pea twigs, you will need a little more time on your seeds, soil and your hands.

v. Paste the asparagus screen on the top of your jar and add running water. Fill the jar with enough cold water to cover the seeds for a few inches (put it at the bottom of the screen). Squeeze around the water a few times and let the water out. Repeat several times until the water is clear and cloudy.

vi. Drain twice a day and rinse your sprouts. Generally, you should rinse any type of sprouts every morning and evening, then drain them well into the drains to promote germination without removing them from the jar.

vii. After the fruits have sprouted, it is normal to add a little water after a few days to break the shell and allow the sprouts to form. Place the jar on your counter. If your bell is not made of stainless steel, remove it to avoid rusting in any way. If your ring is made of stainless steel, you can leave it on the jar throughout the process.

viii. You will control the humidity by cleaning the sprouts from time to time, but you'll need to keep the temperature even higher to promote the sprouts. Keep your sprouts between 50- and 70- degrees F.

ix. If your home is particularly cold at certain times of the year, you may need a heater. An 8-watt heater for tiles placed under the ink will help without overcooking and without ruining the sprouts.

X. Some sprouts, such as radishes, are better sprouts in the dark, but they will need to be exposed to light after sprouting to be green and grow. In general, most sprouts are fine under normal daylight and room temperature conditions.

xi. Make sure your sprouts have some sunlight, especially during the last day or growing 2. It encourages them to become good and green during their final development.

Sprouts growing in inert bags

I. Put 2 tablespoons of sprouted seeds in a bowl or jar. Cover with cold water and let it soak for 8 hours.

ii. Before first use, turn your spirit bag inside out and soak it in boiling water for 5 minutes. Allow to cool and return the bag to its original condition.

iii. Put the soaked seeds in a wet, ready-made anchor bag. Pull off the drawstring. Rinse with fresh water (or set in a bowl of cold water) for 60 seconds. If soaking in a bowl, massage the bag lightly to help prevent slippage and roots from siding into the sidewall.

iv. Drain more water from the bag before hanging for 15 minutes, or until it stops dripping.

v. Place the spirit bag in a bowl after the water has drained to prevent the water from drying out.

vi. Repeat the washing and cleaning process twice a day until the sprouts are fully cooked.

vii. If the vegetables are growing, gently roll the collar of the bag over the last 2 days to reveal the sprouts. Instead of dipping to wash the bag, use a sink sprayer to keep the water on top.

Earth Sprouting

Sprouts can be grown using the traditional soil method, and some believe that because of the high humidity, it is the safest method that can stimulate bacteria or cookies. Soak your sprouts overnight in a jar, making sure the dirty water covers all the seeds. Fill a shallow dish or pot with light potting soil, remove your seeds and place a layer inside the moist soil. Cover with more moist soil and cover the entire container with plastic wrap.

Keep the container in a warm, dark place. Sprouts will start appearing in 3-5 days. When they are long enough, you can cut them with scissors and use them immediately. The cut sprouts will continue to grow and can be harvested later.

Paper towels burst

A very simple method of growing sprouts is between two paper towels. As with other methods, the sprouts should be soaked in water at night in a jar or cup. After getting up, arrange the seeds in two paper towels. Towels should be moisturized frequently to prevent a dry environment. Once the sprouts start, you can increase the length to your desired size and slip with scissors to garnish salads, soups, or main courses. Be careful not to overdo it. The seeds can eventually stick to the mold or paper towels.

Vertical sprouts

i. Clean your kit before use. Use mild soap and warm water.

ii. Place red drainage spout caps on 3 levels of your vertical producer.

iii. Sprinkle 1 tablespoon of sprouted seeds on each growing tray. Stack 3 mounting trays on top of the bucket-shaped bottom tray. This is the tray that will collect all the water flowing through your 3 layers of anchor.

iv. Be sure to locate the sprouts of the red tubes so that they are in a different position on each level. This helps to ensure that water does not run out too quickly.

v. Fill the top basket with water from top to bottom. Keep the lid on and let the water drain through each part completely.

vi. Discard water (or, preferably reuse water plants in the house or in your outdoor garden), place it under your vertical cultivator and keep the grower in direct sunlight.

vii. Repeat the washing and cleaning process twice a day until the sprouts are fully cooked.